MW01257461

Published by:

Traders Accounting
15396 N 83rd Ave,
Suite D100
Peoria, AZ 85381

DISCLAIMER AND LEGAL NOTICES:

While all attempts have been made to verify information provided in this book, neither the Author nor the Publisher assumes any responsibility for errors, inaccuracies or omissions. Any slights of people or organizations are unintentional. If advice concerning legal or related matters is needed, the services of a qualified professional should be sought. This book is not intended for use as a source of legal or accounting advice.

Any reference to persons or businesses, whether living or dead, existing or defunct, is purely coincidental.

VIII.   Setting up legal entities to run you Trading business
- a. Definition of a Legal entity
    - i. Flow Through Entities
        1. Limited Partnership
        2. S Corporation
        3. LLC
    - ii. C Corporation
- b. Combination Entity
    - i. Best structure to use in trading business

IX.   Use of Pension Plans with your entity
- i. 401(k) Plan
- ii. Advantages of Setting up 401(k) Plan

Dear Trader,

We are continually asked for information on the taxation of futures. Many traders do not realize that there is a substantial difference between the taxation of stocks, options on stocks, and the taxation of futures, commodities, and options on indexes. Of even more concern to us is the fact that many of the accountants that are filling out the tax forms for these traders and investors don't appear to know the difference in the taxation either.

This is troublesome for the trader who is making his living actively trading in the futures market place and as a result of hard work and many years of study is successful only to end up giving more of his trading profit to the governments than necessary because of an accountant who does not know the rules. If the trader himself were watching a company to invest in that gave away its profits in this manner he would only short it.

We encourage all that read this booklet to understand that for any active trader, taxes are your biggest expense. It is up to the trader to assume the personal responsibility of understanding and implement a program to minimize the tax burdens. You are to be commending for acquiring this manual.

Our overriding purpose in providing this information is for your use to understand how to formulate an efficient trading plan for yourself. If you place yourself in the position of having to rely on your tax professional to answer all of your questions, you will never know if he truly understands the taxation of futures.

We hope the knowledge you gain from your time with our booklet will be useful to you.

Traders Accounting

April 2014—Phoenix Arizona USA

II. ARE YOU A TRADER OR INVESTOR?

Calculating your taxes is not very simple. You can't just take your income, subtract your expenses, and multiply by a tax rate. That would be too simple, don't you think? The biggest problem, though, is that it would put all of us accountants out of business!

The first step to figuring out your tax situation, is to determine which class of taxpayers you fall within. As a trader, here are your options: You will file as a Dealer in Securities, Investor, or a Trader in Securities.

The Dealer in Securities:

A dealer is a professional middleman. Most likely this isn't your situation.

Let me give you an example of a dealer. You probably have heard of market makers. Market makers are considered Dealers in Securities. Market Makers are individuals and securities firms that use their own capital to buy and maintain an inventory in a specific company's stock. When a Market Maker receives an investor's order to buy shares in a particular stock, it sells those shares to the customer from its existing inventory.

You may also have heard of broker/dealers. These individuals/firms are registered with the Securities and Exchange Commission. Whether you are a market maker or a broker/dealer, to qualify as a dealer in securities in the eyes of the IRS, the bottom line with the IRS is that you must engage in transactions with customers.

Taxation of a Dealer: The timing and character of gains and losses on dealer securities futures contracts (and options on such contracts), is determined under section 1256. Dealer securities futures contracts are subject to mark-to-market treatment, and gains or losses are treated as 60 percent long-term capital gain or loss and 40 percent short-term capital gain or loss.

The Investor

What makes you an investor rather than a trader? Maybe you purchased a few securities a while back and you're planning to hang onto them for a long time. Perhaps for your child's college fund, or for that once-in-a-lifetime trip around the world. Maybe you live on dividend income associated with your investments, or perhaps you're rolling the interest over and creating a nice nest egg for retirement.

In any case, you pay your capital gains tax, and are lucky to realize even a small amount of associated investment deductions. If that sounds like you, then you're counted among the most hardworking American citizens struggling to save money for a rainy day. You are an investor.

Investor Limitations - Deductibility of Investment Expenses

There are many investment expenses, all of which fall into the miscellaneous itemized deduction category and are reported on Schedule A of form 1040—if you're trading as an investor. Unless you're trading as a business, investment expenses are limited, both in scope and to whatever exceeds 2% of your AGI. The IRS' list of investment expenses follows:

Deductible expenses:

- Attorney and accounting fees
- Clerical help and office rent
- Cost of replacing missing securities
- Fees to collect income
- Investment council and advice
- Safe deposit box rental
- State and local transfer taxes
- Investment expenses from pass-through entities

Nondeductible expenses:

- Stockholder's meetings
- Investment related seminars
- Borrowing on insurance
- Tax-exempt income

The Trader in Securities:

Traders occupy a advantageous middle ground that falls in between the limited world of the investor and the highly regulated world of the dealer. On one hand, expenses of your "work" are deductible, and are not dependent on being over 2% of your adjusted gross income, as an investor's expenses are. On the other hand, you don't have to register your business with the government.

An interesting facet of trader taxation is that no real definition of a "trader" exists in the tax code. The data we have now is gleaned from tax court cases, the results of which add to a surprising lack of information available on the topic.

Lack of clarity and research makes for a very ambiguous and fluid definition, so a clear understanding of past court cases is mandatory.

Before we discuss pertinent court cases, a better explanation of trader is warranted. A trader buys and sells securities to take advantage of short-term market changes. Profit comes from price changes, not from dividends and interest. Short-term holding periods mark the trader, with holding periods measured in only days and weeks. And since long-term growth is neither expected nor desired, many traders aren't concerned about which company issues the securities, and therefore forego due diligence research common among investors. A trader's single concern is the profit they make from holding a position for a very short time.

Another telltale sign of a trader is his or her ability to devote substantial amounts of time to their business. According to the IRS, traders need to show an earnest intent to be a trader. Conducting one trade a day does not show serious intent. A trader spends a significant amount of time in trading activities, from managing transactions and conducting strategy sessions, to making frequent trades on a consistent and regular basis. These defining points come from case law, and the IRS will diligently fight what it feels is an unsubstantiated trader election. It's been proven in case after case after case.

What do the Courts Have to Say?

Two early cases speak directly to establishing trader status. In Higgins v. the Commissioner (1941), the Supreme Court denied the deductibility of Higgins' investment expenses. Higgins ran a vast operation, which included offices and employees, who recorded and managed all aspects of his trading activity. Even so, the court concluded that business function did not exist related to Higgins' trading. According to the court, Higgins' business existed solely to record his investments.

Estate of Yaeger v. the Commissioner (1989) is a similar case. Yaeger, according to definition, was the very picture of a trader. Trading was his full-time job, and he made substantial profits buying and selling securities. He equipped himself with offices and a staff, and continuously educated himself regarding financial matters. Yet this was not enough to convince the IRS or the Supreme Court that he was a trader. At issue was the fact that Yaeger held his securities for long periods of time, so the court ruled that Yeager conducted investing activity, and did not run a trading business.

In a more recent case, Fredrick R. Mayer (1994), the court established that even if a trader devotes substantial time to trading activities, trader status would still be denied unless other factors are met. Mayer, like Higgins, ran a vast operation and hired eight money managers to handle his funds. Mayer set the company's goals and monitored his managers closely. He did everything a good businessperson should do to increase profits, yet the IRS and the Tax Court denied him trader status, and disallowed his business deductions. Like Yaeger, Mayer profited from long-term holding periods. Buying frequently negated selling infrequently.

The case of Rudolph Steffler (1995) differs from others because the court denied trader status based on trade infrequency. Steffler conducted a very small number of trades each year, and the Tax Court denied trader status on that ground alone.

Compare Steffler to Higgins, Yaeger and Mayer, where trade frequency was not at issue. In those cases, the court denied trader status due to lengthy holding periods. It's an important distinction, and a significant feature of IRS and court-approved trader status: your intention must be to hold securities for short-term periods, and you must conduct a large number of transactions.

The Tax Court, in the case of Stephen A. Paoli (1991), established a preface to the frequency test. In Paoli, the court focused on the consistency of trading activities. Paoli conducted numerous trades, but most during one particular time of the year. Throughout the remainder of the tax year, Paoli engaged in little to no trading activities. The court ruled that although both the transaction and frequency tests were met, Paoli's activity should have been conducted continuously over the course of the year, just as a business does business all year long.

As we've mentioned, you won't find one specific part of the IRS code that deals with securities traders. However, due to the exponential growth in online trading in the last few years, and the overwhelming advantages conferred upon traders, the IRS has been forced to issue statements regarding the definition. Recently in Revenue Procedure 550, the IRS says that to qualify as a trader in securities:

- You must seek to profit from daily market movements in the prices of securities and not from dividends, interest, or capital appreciation.
- Your activity must be substantial, and
- You must carry on the activity with continuity and regularity.

In addition, the IRS says that the following circumstances must be considered in determining if your activity is a securities trading business:

- Typical holding periods for securities bought and sold.
- The frequency and dollar amount of your trades during the year.
- The extent to which you pursue the activity to produce income for a livelihood.
- The amount of time you devote to the activity.

What does that really tell us? Not much, forcing lawyers and CPAs representing traders to rely on court cases that more clearly define who is eligible for the trader classification. The bottom line is that without adequate definition by the IRS, an individual who files as a trader in securities will always be in jeopardy of losing their privileged status based on a new, overriding court case that raises the bar on required qualifications.

If you are concerned that you may not trade to the level defined by the court cases, you have the option of using a legal entity structure to lock the tax benefits into place. Read later sections covering the use of legal entities.

Conclusion: The dealer is well-defined and highly regulated. The investor is the default classification, and has very prescribed and limited tax breaks. The trader is most likely you - the individual entrepreneur, buying and selling securities for the purpose of making a livelihood. How exactly that looks in the eyes of the IRS is not clearly defined. The benefits however, of taking the initiative to trade as a business are easily understood. Independence, and financial freedom.

III. WASH SALES

The Wash Sale Rules for Traders

Generally, the wash sale rule applies to traders the same way it applies to investors. The difference is that traders have a much harder time keeping records relating to wash sales because they engage in so many transactions.

The wash sale rule basically states that if you sell a stock at a loss and buy replacement stock 30-days before, or 30- days after the sale of the same stock, you can't deduct the loss. This rule does not apply to gains but only to losses. Naturally, the IRS wants to tax all of your gains. The best way to show the impact of the wash sale rule is through the following example:

AN EXAMPLE OF A WASH SALE TRANSACTION

On October 20, 2002 you purchase 1000 shares of Microsoft at $35a share. On December 15, 2002 you sell the 1000 shares in Microsoft at $15 a share and recognize a 20,000 loss. On January 5, 2013 you buy back 1000 shares of Microsoft at $15 a share. Unfortunately, because of the wash sale rules, that $20,000 loss that the taxpayer thought they recognized in 2002 is disallowed.

If you wind up with a wash sale, add your disallowed loss to the basis of your replacement security. Your new basis is the purchase price of the replacement, plus the loss you couldn't take, plus fees related to the security's purchase. This means that your loss is postponed; it's not gone forever. In the above example the taxpayers basis in the Microsoft stock he repurchase on January 5, 2013 would be $35 a share and not the $15 a share he purchased it at.

The definition of replacement stock is not obvious either. The IRS says it can't be "substantially identical" to the security you sold. It's easier to differentiate stocks than it is mutual funds, as no stock is substantially identical to another, even within the same industry. After all, each company differs from others in numerous ways.

Options traders are particularly vulnerable to the Wash Sale Rules. Every single call option, as well as all puts in the money are considered to be replacement stock for wash sale purposes.

With mutual funds though, replacement purchases get sticky. If two different funds track the same index and share virtually identical performance, they're considered substantially identical. Eliminate this problem by buying a mutual fund that moves in the same direction as the one you sold, but one that tracks off a different index.

When you sell the replacement security at a profit later, your basis will be higher, so your gain will lower. The end result? Less tax on a smaller gain. If you sell lower than your replacement security basis, your loss will be larger than it would be if based on the repurchase price alone, so you do get some recovery.

When you make a wash sale, your holding period for the replacement stock includes the period you held the stock you sold. This rule prevents you from converting a long-term loss into a short-term loss.

Most investors run into the wash sale rule only occasionally. If you're an active trader, you're likely to have a large number of wash sales each year. All is not lost; there are several ways to avoid having to deal with the wash sale rules that I will cover next.

TWO WAYS TO AVOID WASH SALES

If you make hundreds or thousands of trades each year, the record keeping required for compliance with the wash sale rule can be nearly impossible. There's several way to eliminate the problem for active traders. The first way to avoid the wash sale rule is to simply wait for 31 days after you sold the stock or option before you buy it back. The second way (which is only available to traders and not investors) is to elect the mark-to-market accounting method.

Full details on the mark-to-market election are beyond the scope of this article at this point, but it's worth pointing out that a trader who makes this election isn't subject to the wash sale rule. There are some other important things you should know if you're thinking of making this election.

- If you make this election, all your trading gains and losses will be treated as ordinary income, not capital gain.
- If you make this election, any stock or other trading asset you hold at the end of the year is "marked to market." This means you report gain or loss as if you sold it at the close of business on the last trading day of the year for its fair market value.
- Once you make this election you're stuck with it. You can revoke it only with the consent of the IRS.

It's easy to see why the wash sale rule doesn't apply if you make this election. All your gains and losses are reported at the end of the year, whether you sell the stocks or not. There's no point in worrying about whether someone sold the stock and bought it back.

ADDITIONAL RULES ABOUT WASH SALES

Below are several different items you need to consider when you deal with the wash sale rules:

- If you bought identical shares within the previous 30 days that aren't replacement shares it is not a wash sale.
- There are mechanical rules to handle the situation where you don't buy exactly the same number of shares you sold, or where you bought and sold multiple lots of shares.
- Your loss may be disallowed if a person who's related to you (or an entity related to you such as an IRA) buys replacement property.
- During the wash sale period if you enter into a contract or option to acquire replacement stock that will be considered a wash sale.
- If you don't sell the replacement stock in the same year, your loss will be postponed, possibly to a year when the deduction is of far less value.
- If you die before selling the replacement stock, neither you nor your heirs will benefit from the basis adjustment.
- You can also lose the benefit of the deduction permanently if you sell stock and arrange to have a related person - or your IRA - buy replacement stock.

IV. MARK-TO-MARKET ACCOUNTING

Beginning in 1997, the tax law has permitted active traders to elect a method of accounting called the mark-to-market method. Many active traders will find this election attractive as a way to make filing simpler — and possibly reduce their taxes.

This is one of the most important decisions you'll make as a trader and your decision will have great ramifications and should not be taken lightly. The rules are fairly complex and will be completely new to most traders. It is very important to read this article thoroughly, and then consult with a knowledgeable tax professional before making your decision.

Mark-to-Market Election

If you're a trader, you may choose whether or not to make the mark-to-market election. You don't automatically get mark-to-market treatment when you file as a trader. And you cannot elect this treatment if you aren't a trader. The election has to be filed by the return due date — without extensions — for the year *before* the year you want the election to be effective. The last day to file the election for the year 2014 was April 15, 2014.

Consequences of the Election

Marking to market - The most obvious consequence of the election is that at the end of each year you must mark your securities to market. What this means is you treat any stocks you hold at the end of the day on December 31 as if you sold them on that day for the current market value. If the stock has gone down, you get to report a loss without actually selling it. If the stock has gone up, you have to report that gain. Your basis for the stock is adjusted to reflect the gain or loss you report, so that you don't report the same gain or loss again when you actually sell the stock.

No wash sales - The wash sale rule doesn't apply to a trader who has made the mark-to-market election. There's a simple logic to this: if all your gains and losses are going to be flushed out on December 31, there's no reason for the tax law to be concerned about wash sales that may occur during the year. For those of you that are investors and non-mark-to-market traders, the wash sale rule is a cumbersome accounting imperative, which says in a nutshell, that if your sell a security (or option) at a loss, and buy that same security (or option) within 30 days before or after the original sale date, than the loss you thought you incurred is disallowed.

Wash sales can be a significant headache for a trader even if they don't affect the amount of tax the trader has to pay. If you make hundreds of trades in the same stock, many of the trades are likely to result in wash sales. At some point, accounting for all the wash sales becomes nearly impossible. Eliminating this concern is a significant benefit of the mark-to-market election.

Ordinary income and loss - If you make the mark-to-market election, your trading gains and losses are converted to ordinary income and loss. You'll report the gains and losses on Form 4797 (sales of business property), not Schedule D (capital gains and losses).

This does *not* mean that your trading gains are now subject to self-employment tax. In a 1998 tax law, Congress clarified that although your trading income becomes ordinary income, it is not self-employment income. This also means you can't use this income to support a contribution to an IRA or other retirement plan.

Traders usually generate all or nearly all of their gains as short-term capital gains, which are taxed at the same rate as ordinary income. In most situations, changing to a system where the trader reports the gains as ordinary income will not have any tax cost. If the trader has capital losses from an investment that isn't part of the trading activity, though, the trader will lose the ability to offset those losses with capital gains from trading.

For many traders, the flip side will be more important. Even good traders sometimes have losing years. When they do, the capital loss limitation rears its ugly head. A trader who has not made the mark-to-market election can deduct only $3,000 of net capital loss, with the excess loss carrying forward only, not back to earlier, profitable years. If you make the election, your trading loss isn't subject to this limitation, and can carry back as well as forward. The difference can be *huge*.

One word of caution for futures and commodity traders is that by electing mark-to-market accounting you will loose the benefit of the 60% long-term capital gain or loss treatment you receive when you trade these types of securities.

You're Stuck With It

Once you make the election, you have to continue to use the mark-to-market method for all future years. You can change the election only with the consent of the Internal Revenue Service, and they generally won't grant this consent if your reason for changing is simply that the election didn't turn out to your advantage. Be sure you know what you're doing before making the election.

Identifying Holdings

Before you make the mark-to-market election, you need to think about identifying any stocks you hold as an investment. Failure to do so could be costly.

What's at Stake - Suppose you're a trader and you make the mark-to-market election. In addition to stocks you trade, you have some stocks you hold as investments. You've held some of these stocks for years, and they've gone up in value a great deal. If these stocks are considered part of your trading business, you'll report ordinary income, not capital gain, when you sell them. Even if you don't sell them, the gain will be treated as ordinary income when you mark to market on December 31. Depending on how much gain you have in your investment stocks, this could be a real disaster.

What You Can Do - The rules permit you to maintain investments that are not part of your trading business. To do this, though, you have to *identify* those investments. In other words, you have to make it clear, up front, which stocks are part of your trading business and which are not. You can't decide later to treat the losers as trading stocks (for ordinary losses) and the winners as investment stocks (to avoid marking to market and get capital gain treatment).

When to Identify - The proposed regulations provide that if you want to identify securities as not being part of your trading business, you must do so on the same day you acquire the security (or enter into or originate your position in the security, in the case of short positions or options). If you hold any investment securities at the time the mark-to-market election becomes effective, presumably you can identify them at that time.

How to Identify - Regulations developed for securities *dealers* provide two ways to identify securities for purposes of these rules. One is to establish a separate account for investment securities, and the other is to clearly indicate on your own records which securities are not part of your trading business.

These rules also apparently apply to securities traders. There's some question in my mind, however, whether the procedure of identifying shares on internal records makes sense for an individual trader. It will be difficult to establish factually that the identification occurred at the proper time, rather than being made up later. *For this reason, I recommend that anyone who makes the mark-to-market election and holds some securities for investment should establish separate accounts for trading and investment activities, taking care never to mix the activities of the two accounts.*

No Connection to Trading Business - Even if you identify securities as investment securities, the IRS can disregard your identification unless you demonstrate by "clear and convincing evidence" that the security has "no connection" to your trading activity. If the IRS rejects your identification, you'll be required to mark the securities to market at the end of the year, and report any gain as ordinary income. It isn't clear what is meant by "no connection" to the trading business. In particular, it isn't clear whether investment securities can be used as collateral for trading margin without being drawn into the mark-to-market regime.

Making the Mark-to-Market Election
Many elections under the Internal Revenue Code are as simple as putting a checkmark in the proper box. That isn't the case for the mark-to-market election. In fact, making the election is a royal pain.

Deadline - The IRS chose an unusual deadline for this election. Most elections are due at the end of the year, when you file your return. This election has to be made by the due date — without extensions — for the *previous* year's tax return. The last day to make the mark-to-market election for the year 2013 was April 15, 2013.

I believe the main reason for this is to prevent taxpayers from choosing the election at a time when they already know whether their trading activity will generate a profit or a loss. Many traders would wait until they have a year with significant trading losses, then file the election for that year to avoid the capital loss limitation. Of course you're stuck with the election for all future years once you make it, but until then you get the benefit of capital gain treatment in profitable years without worrying about the capital loss limitation in a year with poor results.

There's a rule that says a "new taxpayer" (a taxpayer for which no federal income tax return was required for the preceding year) can make the mark-to-market election during the first two months and 15 days of the election year. They make the election by recording it in their books and records rather than by filing an election with the IRS. It appears that this rule was designed for newly formed entities (such as corporations and partnerships). Individuals who start trading after April 15 without forming an entity will apparently have to wait until the following year to make the mark-to-market election.

Making the Election - Making the election is a two-step process (with the second step being in two parts). The first step is to file an election, on or before

the un-extended due date of your tax return for the year *before* the year to which the election applies. If you file your tax return by the regular due date, attach the election to your tax return. If you file on extension, attach the election to your extension request.

Note: You may read elsewhere (as I have) that this election may be filed by itself. The IRS clearly states that the election must be attached to the return or the extension request.

Note: If you filed early you can still make the election if you act by the due date of your return. File an amended return with the election attached.

Here's what an election would look like, assuming it applies beginning in the year 2013 and that it is filed with the original return, not with an extension or amended return:

> John Doe
> SSN 555-55-5555
> Attachment to 2013 Form 1040
> I hereby elect to use the mark-to-market method of accounting under section 475(f) of the Internal Revenue Code for my trade or business of trading securities. The first year for which the election is effective is the taxable year beginning January 1, 2013.
>
> _____
> John Doe

Make appropriate changes if the form is filed for a different year or if it is attached to Form 4868 (individual extension request) instead of Form 1040. IRS guidance doesn't seem to require a separate signature on this statement but I feel more comfortable if the signature is included.

Form 3115 - When you file your return for the year the election is effective, you need to attach Form 3115, an Application for Change in Accounting Methods. You also have to send a copy of Form 3115 to the IRS national office. Because the Form 3115 is a concoction of arcane questions, I highly recommend you consult with a tax professional to assist you in completing the eight-page Form.

The Section 481(a) Adjustment

There's an arcane aspect of the mark-to-market election that confuses many people, including knowledgeable tax professionals. The question is what you

report as the *section 481(a) adjustment* when you file Form 3115 for the mark-to-market election. Here's an explanation of this adjustment.

Purpose of the Adjustment - When you change a method of accounting, it's possible you'll have some items that are either duplicated or omitted because they're treated differently under the two accounting methods. For example, suppose you switched from cash accounting to accrual accounting at the end of 2002. In January, 2013 you paid an expense that relates to the previous year. You can't deduct this amount under the cash method in 2002 because you didn't pay it that year. Likewise, you can't deduct it under the accrual method in 2013 because it relates to the previous year. The section 481(a) adjustment correct for this type of problem. In this case, the adjustment would be an added deduction to make up for the fact that this item fell between the cracks when you changed your method of accounting.

Calculating the 481(a) Adjustment - The mark-to-market election requires you to treat the securities in your trading account as if you sold them for fair market value on the last day of the taxable year, with and resulting gain or loss reported as ordinary income or deduction. Under this method of accounting, you're treated as if you sold your trading securities for fair market value at the end of the year. Your basis for the securities is adjusted for any gain or loss, with the result that for any securities held at the end of the preceding year, basis equals year-end value.

For the last year before the mark-to-market election takes effect, you're still using the normal tax rules to report gain or loss. You don't treat your securities as sold on the last day of the year. Yet under the mark-to-market system, which you're using as of the beginning of the next year, your basis is equal to the value of the securities at the end of the preceding year. That creates the potential for duplication or omission of gain or loss.

Example: At the end of 2000 you held shares with $24,000 basis but value of $26,000. You made the mark-to-market election effective beginning in 2001, and ended up selling these shares for $30,000. You report $4,000 of gain on the sale of the shares, and in addition you have a $2,000 section 481(a) adjustment.
If you held securities at the end of the year preceding your first year using the mark-to-market method, your adjustment is the difference between the value of those securities at the end of the year and your adjusted basis for the securities. Tax professionals looking for authority on this point should review Rev. Rul. 93-76. Although this ruling deals with dealers rather than traders, it explains how the section 481(a) adjustment works in connection with a change to mark-to-market accounting.

V. CAPITAL GAINS

In order to understand the taxation of futures we first need to understand the concept of capital gains. But even before we can get to capital gains, we need to define a capital asset. Whew!

First of all, assets can be classified as either capital or non-capital assets. Capital assets are those held for personal use or for investment. The IRS' list of capital and non-capital assets, which apply to investors and traders, include:

Capital Assets	Non-Capital Assets
▪ Investments	▪ Sales to customers
▪ Your home	▪ Property used in business
▪ Furnishings	▪ Accounts and notes receivable
▪ Automobile	▪ Hedging transactions
▪ Coin and stamp collections	▪ Business supplies
▪ Jewelry	▪ Inventory

Capital assets will be the focus of our discussion on capital gains and losses, as non-capital assets produce ordinary income when sold, and are taxed as such.

Sales of Capital Assets

Just because an asset is considered capital doesn't mean you can deduct a loss on its sale. Losses on personal capital assets cannot be deducted. If for some reason, you sell your new Jaguar and take a $10,000 loss on the sale, it's not deductible. If your gain is $10,000 though, watch out. The IRS wants—and takes—every last tax dollar it can.

Once you decide that the asset you sold is capital, determine if the gain or loss is short-term or long-term in nature. A short-term holding period is one year or less, and a long-term holding period is over one year. The day you acquire the capital personal property counts as day one, and the day you dispose of the property is the last day. For securities, the day after the trade date is considered day one.

Capital activities are reported to the IRS on Form 1099-B, which should be supplied to you. If you've sold securities, it'll come from your broker. These figures are then reported on Schedule D, which accompanies your tax return. Long-term capital assets are subject to a maximum capital gains tax rate of 20% (10% for individuals in the 10% or 15% tax bracket). A lower rate of 8% (for

individuals in the 10% or 15% tax bracket) may apply when the asset was held for more than five years.

Amidst all your trading activities, you'll run into three possible gain/loss scenarios, other than straight gains:

1. Short-term gains and short-term losses
2. Long-term gains and long-term losses
3. Short-term gains and losses and long-term gains and losses

How to Handle Short-term Gains and Short-term Losses

Short-term gains and losses are netted together to produce a net short-term capital amount. If your losses are larger than your gains, the net will be a loss, which is limited to $3,000 on your tax return. If your loss is greater than $3,000, you can carry it over to the following year, while retaining its character as a short-term loss.

If gains are larger than losses, the net effect is a gain, which is taxed as ordinary income. If the gain and loss are identical, you break even on your trading, with no tax effect.

How to Handle Long-term Gains and Long-Term Losses

Long-term gains and long-term losses are also netted together to produce one long-term amount. Netted gains are taxed at a maximum rate of 20%, but netted long-term losses are treated similar to netted short-term losses. Your loss is limited to $3,000 in the current year, with any unused loss being carried forward into the next year. The character of the long-term loss remains, and is considered long-term for future year calculations.

How to Handle Short-Term and Long-Term Gains and Losses

If you find yourself with short-term and long-term gains and losses simultaneously, net your short-term gains/losses together, and net your long-term gains/losses together. Then, net the results of both together. If you're left with a gain, it's taxed at its short or long term rate. If the gain consists of a short-term and a long-term gain, each portion is taxed at its applicable rate. If you're left with a loss, the $3,000 loss limitation still applies. Use the short-term portion of the loss first, leaving the long-term portion (along with any unused short-term loss) available for a carryover if you exceed the $3,000 limitation.

It's also possible to wind up with a mixture of short- and long-term gains and losses. When this happens, the larger gain or loss rules. Your four possible results and how to report them are:

1. If your short-term gain is greater than your long-term loss, take a short-term gain.
2. If your short-term loss is greater than your long-term gain, take a short-term loss that is limited to $3000, with the balance being carried over as a short-term loss.
3. If your long-term gain is greater than your short-term loss, take a long-term gain, taxed at 20%.
4. If your long-term loss is greater than your short-term gain, take a long-term loss that is limited to $3000, with the balance being carried over as a long-term loss.

Examples of Short-Term and Long-Term Gains and Losses

Example: John trades both short and long term positions throughout the year. John has no other income. At the end of the year John has a total of $12,000 in long term gain from the positions you sold. John also traded short term and netted $14,000 in short term gain.

Calculation: Long term gains = $12,000 x 5% = $600 (5% because he is in one of the two lower marginal tax rates. His tax on his long term gains would be $600. Short term gains = $14,000 x 10% = $1,400.

———————————————————————

Example: Benjie traded all year and had the following results: She sold some long term positions she had held for 2 years for a $20,000 gain. She traded short term futures all year and lost $20,000.

Calculation: The two different capital gains would net out to $0 and there would be no tax due.

———————————————————————

Example: Sarahlyn traded all year and had the following results. She sold some long term positions she had held for 3 years for a

$20,000 gain. She traded short term futures all year and lost $30,000.

Calculation:
Her capital loss exceeds her total capital gain, and therefore she would show a net $10,000 loss. She would only be able to deduct $3,000 from her tax return because of the capital loss rules.[1]

How Basis Affects Your Gain or Loss

Your adjusted basis in the capital asset determines your gain or loss. Basis is the price you originally paid for the asset, and the adjusted basis is your original cost or other basis plus additions such as selling expenses to transfer the property to a new owner, or capital improvements in the case of a home, and minus deductions such as depreciation and casualty loss.

In the case of securities, if your broker charges you to conduct trades, his or her expenses are subtracted from your gain (or added to your loss). Your adjusted basis less the selling price is your gross gain or loss. When your broker sends you Form 1099 at the end of the year, read it carefully. Some brokerage firms record gross gain or loss, and some record net gain or loss. Regardless of how it's reported, use net gain or net loss to calculate your taxes.

For tax purposes, a capital asset is generally any property held as an investment, except that rental real estate is generally not a capital asset because it is treated as a trade or business asset. So, here is the end result: you have your capital assets which increase in value over time – the increase in value is called a capital gains – that capital gain is taxed at a specific rate that depends on the length of time you held the capital asset.

There are two different tax categories for capital gains; long term and short term. Each is taxed at different rates.

How are securities identified for tax purposes?

Generally you will be deemed to have sold the securities which were acquired, by a first-in, first out (FIFO) method.[2] However if you wish to "identify" purchases and sales differently than the FIFO method, you are generally able to identify the

---

[1] IRC Sec. 1211 (b)
[2] Treas. Reg §1.1012-1 (c) (1)

lot from which the securities being sold originated in to determine your tax basis and holding period.

Generally, identification of different lots is determined by the certificate delivered to the buyer. The security represented by the certificate is deemed to be the security sold or transferred. However, most of us never take control of our certificates from our broker.

How can we identify different lots if it makes tax sense for us to do so?

There are several exceptions to the general rule of adequate identification. One occurs when the securities are left in the custody of the broker or other agent. If the seller specifies to the broker which securities to sell or transfer, and if the broker or agent sends a written confirmation of the specified securities within a reasonable time, then the specified securities are the securities sold or transferred, even though different certificates are delivered to the buyer or other transferee.[3]

How is an individual taxed on capital gains and losses?[4]

Although there are some significantly complex formulas involved in figuring long term capital gains, generally the maximum capital gains rate on adjusted net long term capital gain will be 0% to the extent an individual is taxed in the first two individual marginal tax rates, 15% to the extent the individual is taxed in the next three marginal rates,[5] and 20% to those taxed at the highest marginal rate. Please see Table V.I for further information.[6]

---

[3] Treas. Reg. §1.1012-1 (c) (3)(i)

[4] Please be aware that there are many complex formulas involved in capital gain treatment, there are rules for different asset gains, and there are rules concerning five year gain as well as other rules that a taxpayer or his accounting professional must be aware of in order to prepare any tax documentation. For discussion purposes in this document we will only cover the tax rules that generally come into play for active traders in the markets.

[5] These rates are due to the new tax legislation passed by congress and signed into law in May 2013. Please note that the long term rates are intended to stay at this rate through 207 and will go to 0% for the lowest two income tax brackets in the year 2008, without future changes.

[6] These rates are due to the new tax legislation passed by congress and signed into law in May 2003. Please note that the long term rates are intended to stay at this rate through 207 and will go to 0% for the lowest two income tax brackets in the year 2008, without future changes.

Individual Tax Brackets							
	Single Filers	$0 to $8,925	$8,925 to $36,250	$36,250 to $87,850	$87,850 to $183,250	$183,250 to $398,350	$400,000 and up
	Married Joint Filers	$0 to $17,850	$17,850 to $72,500	$72,500 to $146,400	$146,400 to $223,050	$223,050 to $398,350	$450,000 and up
	Head of Household Filers	$0 to $12,750	$12,750 to $48,600	$48,600 to $125,450	$125,450 to $203,150	$203,150 to $398,350	$425,000 and up
Ordinary Income	Is Taxed At:	10.00%	15.00%	25.00%	28.00%	33.00%	39.60%
Long Term Capital Gain	Is Taxed At:	0%	0%	15.00%	15.00%	15.00%	20.00%
Short Term Capital Gain	Is Taxed At:	10.00%	15.00%	25.00%	28.00%	33.00%	39.60%

Table V.1

VI. Other Tax Rules to be Aware Of

Short Sales

What is a short sale? What is meant by the expression "short against the box"?

In a short sale an individual contracts to sell stock (or other securities) that he does not own. Because of this he must borrow the stock for delivery to the buyer. He will generally pay a premium for the privilege of borrowing the stock. At a later date, the short seller will repay the borrowed stock to the lender with shares he held, or new shares he has purchased, whichever he chooses.

The act of delivering the stock (or securities) to the lender in repayment for the borrowed shares is referred to as the "closing" of the short sale.

In a sale, "short against the box" the short seller will already own the stock when he places the short sale but chooses to borrow the stock rather than deliver his own

The purchase of a put option is treated as a short sale for some purposes.

In applying the short sale rules, a securities futures contract to acquire property will be treated in a manner similar to the property itself. Thus, for example, the holding of a securities future contract to acquire property and the short sale of property that is substantially identical to the property under the contract will result in the application of the rules under IRC Section 1233 (b). Also you must note that the rule providing that commodity futures are not substantially identical if they call for delivery in different months does not apply.

When and how is a short sale taxed?

Ordinarily whether capital gain or loss on a short sale is long-term or short-term will generally be determined by how long the seller has held the stock he uses to close the sale.[7]

There are other rules that are on the books to prevent individuals from using short sales to convert short-term gains to long-term gains or long-term losses to short-term losses, and to prevent the creation of artificial losses. Because of these and other rules, it is important that a trader who uses short sales in their

---

[7] Treas. Reg. §1.1233-1(a)

trading strategies insure that their tax professional understands short sale taxation.

Constructive Sales

A taxpayer is generally treated as having made a constructive sale of an appreciated financial position if the taxpayer or a related person[8]:
1. Enters into a short sale of the same or substantially identical property
2. Enters into an offsetting notional principal contract[9]
3. Enters into a futures contract or forward contract to deliver the same or substantially identical property.

If a taxpayer holds a long-term position in actively traded stock and enters into a securities futures contract to sell substantially identical stock[10] at a time when the position in the stock has appreciated in value, the constructive sales rules will apply.

Constructive sales bring with them such complicated rules and issues that we recommend you leverage the expertise of Traders Accounting to help you decide whether the rules apply to you or not. The law changed in 1997, as another example of how Uncle Sam likes to close loopholes that benefit traders—and all taxpayers.

According to the Taxpayer Relief Act of 1997, you must now recognize gains, but not losses, upon constructive sales of appreciated financial positions. An appreciated financial position is any interest in stock that would result in a gain if you sold it today. A constructive sale is defined as any of the following transactions in the same or substantially identical property:

- A short sale
- An offsetting principal contract
- A futures contract

---

[8] A person is related to another person with respect to a tranaction if;
1. persons related by family
2. ownership of related entities

[9] With respect to any property, an agreement that includes:
1. a requirement to pay all or substantially all of the investment yield (including appreciation on such property for a specified period and
2. a right to be reimbursed for all or substantially all of any decline in the value of such property. IRC Sec. 1259(d)(2)

[10] While substantially identical stock or securities is not defined in IRC Section 1259 under earlier law the meaning of the term as used for purposes of the short sale rules is the same as that used for the wash sale rule.

If any of these apply to you, you'll need to recognize the gain as if the transaction was conducted at fair market value on the date of the constructive sale. Your holding period changes and begins anew.

There are however, some exceptions. According to the IRS, constructive sales do not apply if you meet all three criteria:

1. You closed the transaction before the end of the 30th day after the end of your tax year, and
2. You held an appreciated financial position throughout a 60-day period, and
3. Your risk of loss was not reduced at any time during a 60-day period.

The tax treatment of constructive sales is so complicated that even tax professionals struggle to understand all the rules. Let Traders Accounting help you pave a clear path through the rocky roads that arise with these sales.

How is a constructive sale of an appreciated financial position treated for tax purposes?

If there is a constructive sale of an appreciated financial position, the taxpayer generally recognizes gain as if the position were sold at its fair market value on the date of the constructive sale.

Straddles

A straddle occurs when you buy both a call option and a put option on the same underlying security, both of which have the same exercise price and expiration date. When you trade straddles, you profit either way—whether the price goes up, or the price goes down. Your goal is to sell the straddle before it expires, just as soon as it brings you the profit you're looking for.

IRS-wise, a straddle is two or more positions that offset each other, reducing risk because the positions are inversely related. If one position is up, the other is down. Positions can be stock or options. Straddles may require a delay in deducting any losses that occur when you sell a position, and may also turn a long-term gain/loss into a short-term gain/loss. And finally, certain expenses that relate to the straddle may not be deductible.

Tax Implications of Straddle Strategies

Generally, you can deduct a loss when you sell one or more straddle positions, but only to the extent that the loss is greater than unrecognized gains you have on offsetting straddle positions. The holding period generally begins no earlier than the date when the straddle ends, meaning when you no longer hold an offsetting position.

Treat your losses as long term if you're holding one or more losing offsetting positions on the date you entered the loss position, and if all gains or losses in the offsetting positions would have been treated as long term if you had sold the positions on the day you entered the loss position. If your loss is disallowed under the straddle rule, it can be carried over to the following year.

Straddle expenses are limited to the amount of your straddle income. Excess amounts are added to the basis of your straddle position.

VIII. FUTURES

What are securities futures contracts?

SINGLE STOCK FUTURES AND NARROW-BASED STOCK INDEX FUTURES

For purpose of income tax rules, the term "securities futures contract" means a contract of sale for future delivery of a single security or a narrow based security index.[11]

A securities futures contract will generally not be treated as a commodity futures contract for purposes of the Internal Revenue Code. Thus, holders of these contracts generally are not subject to the mark-to-market rules of IRC Section 1256 and are not eligible for the 60% long-term capital gain treatment. Instead, gain or loss on these contracts will generally be recognized under the rules relating to the disposition of property as discussed above under the section on capital gains.

These securities will be subject to wash sales, short sales and straddles. Gain or loss on securities futures contracts will be treated under the rules relating to the disposition of the underlying property.

Mark to Market

As indicated above securities futures contracts, or options on such contracts generally are not treated as IRC Section 1256 contracts, however an exception to the general rule exists for traders who have elected Mark to Market as an accounting method.

SECTION 1256 CONTRACTS

WHAT ARE FUTURES? WHAT IS A REGULATED FUTURES CONTRACT?

Generally speaking, a future is a contract which requires performance in the future, to purchase or sell a particular commodity for delivery in the future; a future may be either a futures contract or a forward contract.

Futures Contracts

Futures contracts are bought and sold on at least one of the various commodities or futures exchanges. Once written, futures contracts traded on a domestic exchange are subject to a "various margin under which they are marked to market

---

[11] IRC Sec. 1234B(c)

(m2m) daily. For income tax purposes, a regulated futures contract is a futures contract that is traded on a domestic exchange or on a foreign exchange that employees a cash flow system similar to the variations margin[12] system and is designated by the Secretary of the Treasury[13] as regulated.

A taxpayer who enters into a futures contract to deliver property that is the same as or substantially identical to an <u>appreciated financial position</u>[14] that he holds will generally be treated as having made a <u>constructive sale</u> of that position:

Forward Contracts

Forward contracts in contrast to futures, exist only in the cash market, and are not subject to CFTC regulation, are not standardized as to terms and provisions, and do not involve variations margin. All terms and provisions of a "forward" are subject to negotiation between the buyer and the seller.

Regulated Futures Contracts

For income tax purposes regulated futures contracts are traded on a domestic exchange or on a foreign exchange that employs a cash flow system similar to the variations margin system and is designated regulated by the Secretary of the Treasury.

Besides covering many types of property including the following:
- Agricultural commodities
- T-bills
- Foreign currencies[15]
- Financial instruments

The regulated futures contracts may cover such things not generally though of as property and call for settlement in cash rather than delivery:

---

[12] Variations margin is a daily cash flow system under which each owner of a futures contract declining in value during a trading day must provide additional cash margin equal to the decline in value; conversely an owner of a futures contract increasing in value is permitted to withdraw margin money from his account equal to his profit for that day.

[13] IRC Sec. 1256(g)

[14] What is an "appreciated financial position"?
An appreciated financial position is any position with respect to any stock if there would be a gain were the position sold, assigned or otherwise terminated at its fair market value. The term "appreciated financial position" does not include any position which is marked to market.

[15] FSA 200041006 has an explanation of when a foreign currency contract will be considered a regulated futures contract or listed option and, thus, require m2m treatment.

For tax purposes a regulated futures contract is one of several types of IRC 1256 contracts.

How are regulated futures contracts and other Section 1256 contracts taxed?

Regulated futures contracts are generally taxed under a mark-to-market tax rule that closely corresponds to the daily cash settlement system. As mentioned above regulated futures contracts are one of the types of IRC Section 1256 contracts that are subject to the 1256 rules. Other types of instruments that are taxed in the same manner are foreign currency contracts and nonequity options.

The owner of a regulated futures contract that is part of a tax straddle or a conversion transaction may be subject to different tax rules.

Gains and losses of IRC Section 1256 contracts held for investment are capital gains and losses regardless of the nature of the underlying property.[16]

IRC 1256 contracts are marked to market. Under these rules, gains and losses inherent in these contracts owned by an investor at the end of the year or at any time during the year must be reported annually, even though the gain or loss has not been realized.

Any gain or loss required to be reported by an investor on an IRC Section 1256 contract under the m2m rules is treated as if 40% of the gain or loss is a short term capital gain or loss, and 60% is considered to be a long-term capital gain or loss. The usual holding period rule for determining whether a gain or a loss is short or long term is ignored.

The wash sale rules do not apply to transactions taxed under Section 1256.

An investor who has a net IRC Section 1256 loss for a year may elect to carry such loss back three years and then, to the extent that it is not depleted carry it forward to succeeding years.

---

[16] IRC Sec. 1234A(2); Moody v.; Comm., TC Memo 1985-20

IX. SETTING UP LEGAL ENTITIES FOR YOUR TRADING BUSINESS

What is a Legal Entity?

A legal entity is an organization recognized by the IRS, that has a corresponding Employer Identification Number (whether it has employees or not). There are four structures to choose from: the sole proprietorship, a C-corporation, a flow-through entity such as a limited liability company (LLC) or limited partnership, and a C-corporation that manages a flow-through entity. Which is best? Read on, and find out.

Sole Proprietorships

We'll tell you straight out, setting up a sole proprietorship for your trading business is a bad idea, with the biggest disadvantage being your election of trader status. As we've mentioned, proving trader status is not a well-defined area, and the defining characteristics change all the time. The IRS uses everyday taxpayers (read: sole proprietor traders) to test their theories on how rules will be applied. Selecting a sole proprietorship means that the probability of an audit increases, and the next new tax ruling could change your trader status. That's not a good way to run any business.

There's more bad news regarding sole proprietorships. Personal assets aren't separated from your business assets, so you'll have zero liability protection. Should something go wrong, you could lose your home, and any other personal assets. Tax deductions for your trading business are extremely limited too. As a sole proprietor business owner, you can't make retirement contributions since the income from your trading is not considered self-employment income.

And speaking of income, if you forego the mark to market accounting election, your income is accounted for as a capital gain on Schedule D, but your expenses are reported on Schedule C. Your income is deemed capital, yet expenses are treated as ordinary. This creates an enormous conflict, and appears odd to the average IRS agent that may review your return.

Why is a Legal Entity More Beneficial Than Filing as a Sole Proprietor?

The number one reason you should conduct your trading business within a legal entity is that it solidifies your business activities and expense deductions. If you're like most traders, you'll easily find deductions totaling from $10,000 to $20,000—without even breaking a sweat. And, if you're a trader with substantial losses, and

you're filing under the mark-to-market accounting method, the $3,000 capital loss limitation waiver could be worth tens of thousands of dollars.

If you're not operating under a legal entity, your tax savings are continually in jeopardy. At any moment, a new tax court ruling could re-define the definition of a trader, and throw your entire tax plan into the garbage, with no recourse.

Also, establishing a legal entity for your trading business brings you sound peace of mind. You'll lock in the benefits of the trading business, rather than being at the whim of the IRS. Legal entities, unlike securities traders, are well defined, so you'll be sure of the status conferred upon your business activities and expenses.

Flow-Through Entity: Limited Liability Company

A limited liability company (LLC) is a relatively new entity that affords two key benefits: asset protection for members, and loss deductibility. When you run your trading business under an LLC, your potential loss extends to the capital you paid into the business. And, your assets are protected. An LLC's income, losses, tax deductions and tax credits are passed through to you, the taxpayer. You may fully deduct losses against ordinary income, which again, helps any business just starting out. And as an added benefit, you may set up retirement plans, which are deductible to the business and are not taxed at the individual level. You'll find more on retirement accounts in our bonus materials.

Flow-Through Entity: Limited Partnership

Until the advent of the limited liability company, limited partnerships were the way to go. The benefits of both entities are the same. Your potential loss extends only to the capital you pay into the business, and your assets are protected. The partnership itself is not taxed. As a flow-through entity, income, losses, deductions, and credits are all passed through to you, the taxpayer. And, you don't have to pay self-employment taxes on your income.

Who Should Use Flow-Through Entities for Their Trading Business?

The LLC and limited partnership are perfect for traders who are active, completing more than 15-20 trades per month, who want to write-off their business expenses, and who may want to use a portion of earnings to pay for personal expenses.

The IRS allows both to be regarded as a "pass through" type of tax entity. That Is, the profits or losses pass through the business and are reflected and taxed on the

individual owners' tax returns, rather than being reported and taxed at a separate business level (as with a regular Corporation). The members (partners) of flow-through entities pay tax on their individual share of income, and generally use any losses to offset other personal income.

C-Corporation

A C-corporation may be a great choice if you're doing business as a trader. Since a corporation is a legal entity in its own right, with the right to sue and be sued, and the right to enter into contractual agreements, it, like any other "individual," pays its own taxes. Even better, a C-corporation gives you and other shareholders personal asset protection.

A C-corporation brings you many other benefits as well, such as the ability to amortize pre-existing and start-up expenses, depreciate business assets, and maximize allowable write-offs. In fact, corporate deductions are so wide reaching that frankly, if your expense is ordinary and necessary, it's deductible.

For those who think starting a corporation means starting a company like Microsoft, you'll be pleased to learn that your corporation can be any size. In fact, you need only one person, yourself, to fill the roles of officer, director and shareholder. You can be your own corporation! Your family members may participate in the corporation as well, as you'll soon see.

Of course, corporations have their downsides too, the major one being double taxation. If you form a corporation, its profit is taxed on the corporate level. And when you pay those once-taxed profits out by way of shareholder dividends, the recipient shareholders, i.e. you, must report the payment as dividend income, creating two taxes on the same profit. However, you can easily avoid double taxation if you're a sole owner corporation. Simply use extra funds to invest in another LLC trading vehicle rather than paying out dividends.

Who Should Use the C-Corporation for Their Trading Business?

The C-corporation, by itself, works well if you're looking to grow your wealth by long-term investing rather than using profits for short-term needs. One of the main advantages is that the C-corporation has its own tax brackets. For example, instead of your trading gains being taxed at your personal tax rates, the first $50,000 of profits in your C-corporation are taxed at just 15%. In addition, the C-corporation is unique in that it gives you the ability to write-off 100% of all medical expenses, including long-term care and other related expenditures. If

you're in this situation, the C-corporation may be right for you. (See our later discussion on writing off medical expenses for more information.)

Corporations with a Flow Through Entity:

Limited Liability Company with a C-Corporation as Management

You'll enjoy all the benefits of a C-corporation, including:

- Fully deductible fringe benefits
- No self-employment taxes
- Personal asset protection
- Clear tax laws, with few gray areas

The C-corporation acts as management. It conducts your trades, pays your bills, and enters into agreements for itself and for your LLC. You, and your family members, hold the C-corporations' stock.

The LLC, on the other hand, acts as the trading company, and is the owner of securities traded by your C-corporation. LLC members include you, your family members, and your C-corporation. Because the C-corporation manages the LLC's activity, the only expenses the LLC incurs are commissions, margin and management expenses. And, LLC members may take distributions versus a salary, and avoid payroll taxes. Of course since the LLC is a pass through entity, you'll still pay tax—but later.

The LLC holds your brokerage account, and the LLC's personal asset protection means it can't be seized in the event of a dispute since you personally do not own it—the LLC does.

Even better, since your corporation handles your trading and deducts all trading expenses from its management income, the bulk of your profit is taxed at the lower corporate rate. (For example, the first $50,000 of income to the C-Corp is taxed at 15%.) Now you'll still have to pay tax on dividends (if you issue them), but the only income that passes through to you, as the LLC owner, is income the LLC creates itself.

Who Benefits from Using the C-Corporation in Combination with a Flow-Through Entity?

If you want to use a legal entity for your trading, and you want to take money out of your trading business without paying payroll taxes, and you will be trading less

than 200 trades per year, the C-corporation/LLC combination may be right for you. The C-corporation acts as the manager of the LLC trading business, making all of the trading and business decisions. As such, all of the expenses are run through the corporation. The LLC is used strictly for holding the brokerage account.

Where Should You Locate Your Entity?

Any entity that carries on an active business must be registered with the state where the business is conducted. As a general rule, when an entity has revenue and/or takes business deductions, it's carrying on an active business, and needs to be registered in that state. If you pay payroll to fund your retirement account or medical insurance, you must register your business within the state where you live. In many cases, it's best to set up the entity in the state where you live. In some cases, however, you might want to consider a state that does not tax income (e.g., Nevada).

Which Entity Should You Use for Your Trading Business?

We do not believe that there is any one perfect entity, or entity structure. However, in our experience, the three simplest, most beneficial structures for active traders are a standalone LLC, a standalone C-corporation, or a combination of the C-corporation and the LLC.

As you may be beginning to see (and as you'll see even more later when we discuss deductions), it's important that you trade under the protection of a legal entity in order to convert what are now personal expenses into deductible business expenses.

Which entity is right for you, and will work best with your lifestyle, trading habits and goals? It's a big decision. We at Traders Accounting invite you to leverage our years of trader and entity tax experience. Email us at learn@tradersaccounting.com, or call us at 1-800-938-9513. We'll review your situation and help you determine which entity is right for you. On top of that, we're pros at setting up entities quickly and cost-effectively, and will get your new entity started soon so you can begin realizing the savings.

IX. USE OF PENSION PLANS WITH YOUR ENTITY

The Two Main Reasons Why Active Investors Need to be in Control of Their Own Retirement Account

Reason number one is that most of our wealth is contained in either an IRA or some pension plan. With the funds inside these accounts, our ability to access and invest them as we want are limited. Even though the retirement accounts are our property, we have little to say about how the money is invested. Control is vested in our pension or IRA account trustee who invests our money in what they consider to be "safe" investments like mutual funds and money market accounts.

Over the past couple of years, most of us have found that these "safe investments" are just another name for "how I lost 30% of my retirement account this year." Different people have diverse approaches to both terms "safe" and "investment." We do not believe that an investment should be classified as an investment unless it returns money on equity each year ("ROE"). If it does not do this, it is a liability rather than an investment. If you could use it the way you wished, you would insure an ROE. No one cares as much about your retirement funds as you do. To fund managers, your retirement monies are just a few dollars added to some gigantic mutual fund. These people do not even know what you want to do when you retire or how you want to spend your money; they just trade it because that is how they are paid. Have you seen the salaries some of these people earn even when they lose money for investors?

The second reason is this will allow your trading business the ability to expense out all the monies contributed to the pension plan for each employee! Business expenses directly reduce the amount of tax your business pays. The contribution the business makes to the retirement account is for the employees of your trading business—generally your family members that you have hired to help you with your business. With a qualified retirement account, you may expense up to $40,000 per employee per year into the employee's retirement account and be in complete control of the money!

A Qualified Pension Plan is One of the Most Attractive Tax Shelters Available
If you are self-employed or have your own business entity and you want to grow your retirement account as fast as possible, you need a pension plan. If you invested $10,000 per year for 30 years in a pension at a rate of return of 15%, you would end up with $5,000,000 after 30 years compared to only $1,500,000 if the money you made was subject to taxes, a difference of $3,500,000!

The Key is to be the Trustee for Your Own 401(k):

When you move your retirement account into a 401(k), owned by your trading entity, **you become the trustee**. Place your total funds into a bank account owned by your 401(k).

Tax Reduction For Your Business Entity:
When a business contributes money to a pension plan, the money is deductible to the business. The business is funding employee retirement with pre-tax dollars. This lets your business pay fewer dollars in taxes. Funding an employee pension plan is one of the best ways to reduce business taxes and increase employees' retirement monies. Imagine loading up your retirement assets with pre-tax dollars. What a fantastic way to ensure a great retirement!

No Tax Liability To The Employees:
Perhaps the best part of having your business set up a pension plan is that the money put into the plan is not considered income to the employee until he or she withdraws it upon retirement. Instead of the retirement money growing, due to capital gains taxes, your retirement assets grow exponentially within the tax-deferred pension plan. Setting up a pension plan minimizes the business tax liability while you and your family (the employees) reap the benefits of tax-deferred growth for retirement and college expenses.

Up To $51,000 Can Be Contributed:
Beginning in the year 2002, subject to regulation, the business can contribute as much as 25% of your employee's salary into the pension plan, a maximum of $51,000 per employee. Just imagine how that amount would grow if it were not subject to taxes

Supercharge Your Yearly Investment:
In 2013, when using a 401(k) Profit Sharing plan for your trading business, you will be able to contribute more than 25% of your earned income. The rules for a 401(k) are the same for the maximum contribution of $51,000. The company can contribute up to 25% of its employee's income. The employee can contribute up to $17,500 per year.

Earnings Within The Plan Accumulate Tax-Deferred
The pension plan is a tax-deferred vehicle. Since no taxes are paid on the funds prior to being contributed to the plan, the contributions within the plan will grow more rapidly than funds contributed in an after-tax basis.

You Control Investments-Trade on Margin or Trade Options or Short!

You will serve as the trustee of the pension plan. You will have full control to invest your retirement account as you see fit. There are few limits on the types of investments you can make. Your investments can be in any security market, in real estate, or any other prudent investment. Trading on margin may cause tax to be due on profit made from the margin—UBTI Unrelated Business Taxable Income.

Borrow From Your Plan

Subject to regulation, the business is allowed to loan money out of the pension plan with no penalties or taxes incurred. How would you like to be able to access your pension monies through such a loan? The ability to borrow from your plan is an excellent vehicle to provide liquidity in a time of need, to fund a business, or any investment purpose. The interest you will pay on the loan flows into your retirement account where it is tax-deferred.

Roll Over Your Existing Retirement Investments

One of the interesting aspects of the new tax law is that you can roll over almost all bona-fide retirement accounts into a qualified plan. This means you will be able to take all of your existing qualified plans, all of your IRAs and roll them into one qualified plan with you as the trustee. This gives you greater control of your retirement funds. You will then also be able to continue funding this retirement account with funds from your business as discussed above.

Control Timing Of Distributions

You can take retirement distributions from your pension plan as early as age 55 or as late as the age you finally stop trading. Subject to regulations you as trustee will be in complete control of your retirement account!

Asset Protection of your Retirement Money

Recently, we have seen an erosion of the protection of people's IRAs from state laws and IRS mandates. The O. J. Simpson case illustrated how a qualified pension plan is almost completely protected from outside lawsuits and liens against the owner of the plan. This will give you the protection you need and deserve for your retirement monies.

Who needs a Qualified Retirement Plan?
Two types of forward thinking individuals need to have this plan:

1. Someone with an IRA or other retirement plan from a previous employer who wants to take control of their life and their retirement funds

—OR-

2. Someone with a closely held, active, business who wants to build some of the business profits into wealth for family use, as well as creating tax advantages for themselves.

If you are in either of these situations please call us at once to work with our attorneys who specialize in setting up 401(k) plans. Let us work with you to maximize your future wealth!

What Are Your Next Steps?

We do not believe that there is any one perfect entity, or entity structure. However, in our experience, the three simplest, most beneficial structures for active traders are a standalone LLC, a standalone C-corporation, or a combination of the C-corporation and the LLC, and in most cases, the use of a 401(k) pension plan.

As you may be beginning to see, it's important that you trade under the protection of a legal entity in order to convert what are now personal expenses into deductible business expenses.

Which entity is right for you, and will work best with your lifestyle, trading habits and goals? It's a big decision. We at Traders Accounting invite you to leverage our years of trader and entity tax experience. Email us at learn@tradersaccounting.com, or call us at 1-800-938-9513. We'll review your situation and help you determine which entity is right for you. On top of that, we're pros at setting up entities quickly and cost-effectively, and will get your new entity started soon so you can begin realizing the savings.

Glossary

Accelerated Depreciation: A depreciation method that expenses a larger amount in earlier years, and less in future years.

Adjusted Gross Income: The bottom figure of page one of Form 1040, also known as AGI, which is used as a base for your personal deductions, as well as your tax liability.

Amortize: To write-off a portion of an intangible asset's value over time. Same concept as depreciation but used when writing off intangible assets, such as goodwill and start-up costs.

Asset: A resource that is expected to bring future benefit to a business.

Audit: Being questioned by an IRS agent about a tax return.

Basis: Ownership value in an asset. Typically calculated as your original cost, plus or minus various other factors.

Business Intent: Having a clear vision and purpose of running a business.

Business Use Vehicle: A vehicle used for business purposes.

Capital Appreciation: The increase in the value of a capital asset.

Capital Asset: Asset held for personal use or investment, such as jewelry, your business or home.

Capital Gain: The profit from selling a capital asset.

Capital Gain Tax: The tax charged on profits from the sale of a capital asset.

Capital Loss Carryover: A capital loss that is not used up in one year, which can be carried forth into following years.

Corporation: A business entity that owns shares of stock.

CPA: A Certified Public Accountant.

Credit: A dollar for dollar reduction in taxes owed; reduces your tax directly.

Day trader: A person who profits from buying and selling securities on a daily basis.

Deductible: Used in reference to expenses, which are subtracted from business profits or AGI to determine a taxable, or net profit, amount.

Depreciation: A write-off of a portion of an asset's value over time.

Dividends: A distribution of earnings to stockholders based on shares owned.

E-Filing: The electronic filing of a tax return, either by the Internet or by modem.

Fair Market Value: The value of an asset in the retail environment.

Financial Diary: A notebook used to record all financial matters pertinent to taxes.

Flow-through Entity: A business where profits and losses pass to the business owner's tax return, rather than being taxed directly.

Holding Period: The length of time a security is owned.

Hope Scholarship: A tax credit of up to $1500 for a student in college during their first two years.

Income: Earnings from business activities.

Interest: The amount charged by a lender to a borrower for use of funds.

Investor: One who sets aside funds or other assets in hopes of long-term growth and profit.

Legal Entity: An organization recognized by the government to conduct business.

Lifetime Learning Credit: A credit for up to $1000 per year of student tuition fees.

Limited Liability Company: A business entity with the tax characteristics of a partnership and the asset protection of a corporation.

Limited Partnership: A business entity in which the partner(s) liability is limited to their initial investment.

Loss: Expenses greater than income, or fair market value less than basis.

Mark to Market Accounting: A method of valuing assets as if they were sold at year-end at Fair Market Value and then repurchased the next day.

Medical Expense Reimbursement Plan: A plan whereby the business owner reimburses employees for medical expenses.

Net Investment Income: The excess of investment income over investment expense.

Normal Expense: An expense incurred in the normal course of business; one incurred by most others doing similar activities.

Not-for-Profit Activity: A business classified as a hobby.

Non-capital expense: An expense classified as ordinary, and therefore deductible.

Ordinary Income: Various forms of income designated by the IRS to be taxed at a non-capital rate.

Ordinary Expense: An expense incurred in the normal course of business.

Partnership: Two or more persons doing business together, with or without a formal agreement.

Partnership Agreement: The agreement made by partners, which spells out each partner's percentage of profits and losses, as well as other partnership business duties.

Passive Activity: An activity that is not actively participated in.

Passive Income: Income from an activity not actively participated in.

Passive Loss: A loss from an activity not actively participated in.

Personal Use Vehicle: A vehicle not used for business purposes.

Realized Gain: A gain that is recognized for tax purposes.

Realized Loss: A loss that is recognized for tax purposes.

Self-employment Tax: Social security and Medicare taxes charged to a self-employed business owner based on net income.

Short-term Gain: Profits occurring from the sale of an asset with a holding period of less than one year.

Sole Proprietorship: An unincorporated business with one owner.

Standard Mileage Rate: An allowable rate per mile dictated by the IRS to use for calculating automobile expenses.

Tax Code: The tax rules and regulations dispensed by the IRS.

Taxable Income: Income that is taxable to the IRS from page two of Form 1040, or the net profit of a business.

Trader: An investor who makes short-term investments on a daily, frequent and regular basis.

Wash Sale: A sale in which a sold security is repurchased 30 days before or after the sale of the same or similar security.

Trader Status: The election an individual makes to be treated as a trader rather than an investor for tax purposes.

Unrealized Gain: A gain that is not recognized for tax purposes.

Unrealized Loss: A loss that is not recognized for tax purposes.

Write-off: To transfer the balance, or a portion of the balance, in an asset account to an expense account. Also refers to deductible expenses.

Made in the USA
Las Vegas, NV
26 September 2024

95810840R00031